# Prayer *Changes* Things

By T.J. Rohleder

A Collection of the Very Best Thoughts Ever Written About the Power of Prayer.

# Prayer *Changes* Things

We hope you enjoy these quotes
we compiled from several sources.
If you believe any of these quotes are incorrect
or protected by copyright, please let us know.

Copyright ® MMXXI Terence Storm Publishing.

All rights reserved. No part of this book may be used or reproduced in any manner whatsoever without the written permission of the publisher. Printed in the United States of America. For information address:

Terence Storm Publishing
P.O. Box 198
Goessel, Kansas 67053

ISBN 1-933356-64-2

# INTRODUCTION
# Why Pray?

### By T.J. Rohleder

Many studies have looked at how health and well-being are influenced by having spiritual beliefs, praying, and attending religious services, and these have found a wide range of benefits.

**Here are just 12 of the amazing benefits of prayer:**

1. **Becoming More Forgiving** – Two studies at Florida State University found that praying for a person increases your ability to forgive that person. In one study, people who prayed for a romantic partner harbored fewer vengeful thoughts and emotions and were more ready to forgive and move on after a conflict. In another study, men and women prayed for the well-being of a close friend, daily for four weeks, while others simply thought positive thoughts about their friend. Those who prayed were more willing to forgive, not only the friend but other people in general. Forgiveness is associated with better overall health and satisfaction with life.

2. **Achieving Goals More Effectively** – Researchers at the University of Miami analyzed more than eight decades of research and found that prayer and other religious practices improve the ability to pursue and achieve long-term goals. Prayer affects regions

of the brain that improve self-control, and people who view their goals as sacred put more effort and energy into attaining them.

3. **Living a Longer Life** – Numerous studies have found that people who are religious are likely to live a longer life. For example, an analysis of 42 studies with a total of more than 125,000 people found that in addition to private prayer, attending religious services, and being involved in other church activities predicted a longer and healthier lifespan.

4. **Reducing Financial Strain** – A study of more than 800 older people found that faith and attendance at religious services offset the emotional toll of financial strain. Researchers at the University of Michigan found that prayer increases gratitude which, in turn, reduces the negative impact of financial difficulties.

5. **Increasing Happiness and Financial Satisfaction** A University of South Florida study of 1,413 adults found that those who are the most religious, in terms of prayer with a positive focus, attendance at church services, and using their faith to deal with day-to-day problems in a positive way, are happier and more satisfied with their financial situation.

6. **Protecting Against Stress** faced with stressful events, older people with strong personal religious beliefs do not experience significantly elevated blood pressure, according to a study at Utah State University. Their reaction is much like that of people who are 30 or 40 years younger.

7. **Decreasing Alcohol Abuse** People who frequently pray and regularly attend church

services are less likely to abuse alcohol, according to a Duke University study of nearly 3,000 people between the ages of 18 and 97. Watching or listening to religious television or radio programs does not have the same impact.

8. **Kids Doing Better in School** Kids who are involved in church activities have higher educational expectations and are likely to do better in math and reading. The National Survey of Children's Health found that school-aged children who attend religious services at least once a month are half as likely to repeat a grade than those who attend less frequently.

9. **Significantly Lowering Health Risks** Numerous studies have shown that people who hold and practice religious beliefs with a positive outlook have lower health risks, assessed in studies with the same types of tests used in medical check-ups, including weight, blood pressure, cholesterol, and blood sugar. For example, in a study of nearly 6,000 Californians between the ages of 21 and 75, attending weekly religious services reduced risk of death and disease for women to the same extent as not smoking, not abusing alcohol, or being physically active. Benefits for men, although notable, were not as pronounced.

10. **Improving Family Relationships** Compared to non-religious teenagers, those who find meaning and importance in religion, and continue to do so during their teen years, experience a better relationship with each parent. And, the whole family has a more satisfying relationship. However, when parents try to enforce beliefs that

the children do not share or easily accept, relationships can worsen.

11. **Encouraging a Healthy Lifestyle** At the University of Texas, researchers examined whether people who frequently attend religious services take more action to maintain good health, compared to those who attend less frequently or not at all. Among 1,504 Texas adults, they found that those who attended church once a week were approximately 60 percent more likely to get regular physical and dental exams and to routinely take vitamins; about half as likely to go to bars; twice as likely to regularly use seat belts; 73 percent more likely to walk; 84 percent more likely to do strenuous exercise; and 49 percent more likely to get restful sleep. Those who attended religious services more than once per week were half as likely to smoke and nearly three times as likely to drink alcohol only occasionally or moderately, rather than being heavier drinkers.

12. **Having a Happier Marriage** Couples who share religious beliefs, practices, and affiliations are happier than those with different or no religious orientation, according to a study of nearly 1,400 Americans between the ages of 18 and 59, conducted by the National Marriage Project at the University of Virginia. The happiest couples think, discuss, and practice their beliefs in the home, rather than only attending church services. Earlier research has identified three ways in which religion enhances marriages: By promoting ethical behavior (the Golden Rule) and forgiveness; by providing a family-oriented social network; and by bringing a sense of

meaning and purpose to life, which increases resilience to stress.

## The Prayer Pitfall

Most of the time, prayer focuses on positive things such as giving thanks or seeking strength, support, or guidance. It reduces stress, anger, and hostility, and has a beneficial effect on one's physical and emotional health. However, when prayer has negative connotations, the effect is detrimental. At Duke University, a study of nearly 600 hospital patients, published in the Archives of Internal Medicine, found increased risk of death among those with negative perspectives such as: "Wondered whether God had abandoned me," "Questioned God's love for me," and "The devil made this happen." Another study, published in the Journal of Palliative Medicine, looked at nearly 200 breast cancer patients. It found that mental well-being, depression, and life satisfaction decreased significantly among women who felt abandoned by or angry at God. Several studies at Case Western Reserve University, published in the Journal of Personality and Social Psychology, found that anger at God and other negative religious perspectives led to problems recovering from the death of a loved one.

Negative views included holding God responsible for severe harm, attributions of cruelty to God, difficulty finding meaning, and seeing oneself as a victim. Prayer which fosters compassion and a loving attitude reduces a harmful stress response in the brain.

Please focus on these reasons as you read this small book. Do this and you will be letting prayer change things in your life.

# Prayer *Changes* Things

"Prayer is not asking. It is a longing of the soul. It is daily admission of one's weakness. It is better in prayer to have a heart without words than words without a heart."
— *Mahatma Gandhi*

"The function of prayer is not to influence God, but rather to change the nature of the one who prays."
— *Soren Kierkegaard*

"I cannot believe in a God who wants to be praised all the time."
— *Friedrich Nietzsche*

"Do not pray for an easy life, pray for the strength to endure a difficult one"
— *Bruce Lee*

"Most of us would prefer, however, to spend our time doing something that will get immediate results. We don't want to wait for God to resolve matters in His good time because His idea of 'good time' is seldom in sync with ours."
— *Oswald Chambers*

"To pray is to build your own house.

To pray is to discover that Someone else
is within your house.

To pray is to recognize that it is
not your house at all.

To keep praying is to have no house
to protect because there is only One House.
And that One House is everybody's Home.

In other words, those who pray from the heart
actually live in a very different and ultimately
dangerous world. It is a world that makes the
merely physical world seem anemic,
illusory, and relative."
— *Richard Rohr*

"Forgive me my nonsense as I also forgive the
nonsense of those who think they talk sense."
— *Robert Frost*

"If the only prayer you said was
thank you, that would be enough."
— *Meister Eckhart*

"Prayer is not asking. Prayer is putting oneself
in the hands of God, at His disposition, and
listening to His voice in the depth of our hearts."
— *Mother Teresa*

"I think the reason we sometimes have the false sense that God is so far away is because that is where we have put him. We have kept him at a distance, and then when we are in need and call on him in prayer, we wonder where he is. He is exactly where we left him."
— *Ravi Zacharias*

"Let us never forget to pray. God lives. He is near. He is real. He is not only aware of us but cares for us. He is our Father. He is accessible to all who will seek Him."
— *Gordon B. Hinckley*

"I have been driven many times upon my knees by the overwhelming conviction that I had no where else to go. My own wisdom and that of all about me seemed insufficient for that day."
— *Abraham Lincoln*

"Why must people kneel down to pray? If I really wanted to pray I'll tell you what I'd do. I'd go out into a great big field all alone or in the deep, deep woods and I'd look up into the sky—up—up—up—into that lovely blue sky that looks as if there was no end to its blueness. And then I'd just feel a prayer."
— *L.M. Montgomery*

"You pray in your distress and in your need; would that you might pray also in the fullness of your joy and in your days of abundance."
— *Kahill Gibran*

"The Simple Path
Silence is Prayer
Prayer is Faith
Faith is Love
Love is Service
The Fruit of Service is Peace"
— *Mother Teresa*

"The more you pray, the less you'll panic. The more you worship, the less you worry. You'll feel more patient and less pressured."
— *Rick Warren*

"In prayer it is better to have a heart without words than words without a heart. "
— *John Bunyan*

"Don't worry if people think you're crazy. You are crazy. You have that kind of intoxicating insanity that lets other people dream outside of the lines and become who they're destined to be."
— *Jennifer Elisabeth*

"There is a God, there always has been. I see him here, in the eyes of the people in this [hospital] corridor of desperation. This is the real house of God, this is where those who have lost God will find Him... there is a God, there has to be, and now I will pray, I will pray that He will forgive that I have neglected Him all of these years, forgive that I have betrayed, lied, and sinned with impunity only to turn to Him now in my hour of need. I pray that He is as merciful, benevolent, and gracious as His book says He is."
— *Khaled Hosseini*

"Is prayer your steering wheel or your spare tire?"
— *Corrie Ten Boom*

"God, grant me strength to accept those things I cannot change."
— *Dan Brown*

"May God break my heart so completely that the whole world falls in."
— *Mother Teresa*

"I have so much to do that I shall spend the first three hours in prayer."
— *Martin Luther*

"Any concern too small to be turned into a prayer is too small to be made into a burden."
— *Corrie Ten Boom*

"In the end, the number of prayers we say may contribute to our happiness, but the number of prayers we answer may be of even greater importance."
— *Dieter F. Uchtdorf*

"In the silence of the heart God speaks. If you face God in prayer and silence, God will speak to you. Then you will know that you are nothing. It is only when you realize your nothingness, your emptiness, that God can fill you with Himself. Souls of prayer are souls of great silence."
— *Mother Teresa*

"Sometimes I go to God and say, "God, if Thou dost never answer another prayer while I live on this earth, I will still worship Thee as long as I live and in the ages to come for what Thou hast done already. God's already put me so far in debt that if I were to live one million millenniums I couldn't pay Him for what He's done for me."
— *A.W. Tozer*

"We tend to use prayer as a last resort, but God wants it to be our first line of defense. We pray when there's nothing else we can do, but God wants us to pray before we do anything at all.

"Give me the Love that leads the way
The Faith that nothing can dismay
The Hope no disappointments tire
The Passion that'll burn like fire
Let me not sink to be a clod
Make me Thy fuel, Flame of God"
— *Amy Carmichael*

"Be not forgetful of prayer. Every time you pray, if your prayer is sincere, there will be new feeling and new meaning in it, which will give you fresh courage, and you will understand that prayer is an education."
— *Fyodor Dostoevsky*

"Prayer may just be the most powerful tool mankind has."
— *Ted Dekker*

"Do not pray for easy lives. Pray to be stronger men.
— *John F. Kennedy*

"Prayer for Love
Thank You, Creator of the Universe
for the gift of Life you have given me,
Thank You for giving me everything that I have ever needed,
Thank You for the opportunity to experience
this beautiful body and this wonderful mind,
Thank You for living inside me with all
Your Love and Your pure and boundless Spirit,
with Your warm and radiating Light.
Thank You for using my words, for using my eyes,
for using my heart to share your love wherever I go.
I love You just the way you are and because
I am your creation, I love myself just the way I am.
Help me to keep the Love and the Peace in my
Heart and to make that Love a new way of life,
that I may live in Love the rest of my life.
Amen."
— *Don Miguel Ruiz*

"I prayed for freedom for twenty years, but
received no answer until I prayed with my legs."
— *Frederick Douglass*

"The man who prays is the one who thinks that god
has arranged matters all wrong, but who also thinks
that he can instruct god how to put them right."
— *Christopher Hitchens*

"Prayer is not an old woman's idle amusement. Properly
understood and applied, it is the most potent instrument of action."
— *Mahatma Gandhi*

"She knew that was not an honest prayer, and she did not
linger over it. The right prayer would have been, Lord . . .
I am miserable and bitter at heart, and old fears are rising
up in me so that everything I do makes everything worse."
— *Marilynne Robinson*

"Help" is a prayer that is always answered. It doesn't matter how you pray--with your head bowed in silence, or crying out in grief, or dancing. Churches are good for prayer, but so are garages and cars and mountains and showers and dance floors. Years ago I wrote an essay that began, "Some people think that God is in the details, but I have come to believe that God is in the bathroom."
— *Anne Lamott*

"Many people pray to be kept out of unexpected problems. Some people pray to be able to confront and overcome them."
— *Toba Beta*

"Those who pray for your downfall are concentrating negative thoughts towards you, without being aware of the slippery ground in which they are standing, which could lead to their downfall."
— *Michael Bassey Johnson*

"The wise man in the storm prays God not for safety from danger but for deliverance from fear."
— *Ralph Waldo Emerson*

"Never pray for justice, because you might get some."
— *Margaret Atwood*

"Those blessings are sweetest that are won with prayer and worn with thanks."
— *Thomas Goodwin*

"The Ego is a veil between humans and God'. In prayer all are equal."
— *Rumi*

"The inner voice is something which cannot be described in words. But sometimes we have a positive feeling that something in us prompts us to do a certain thing. The time when I learnt to recognise this voice was, I may say, the time when I started praying regularly."
— *Mahatma Gandhi*

"Pray, hope, and don't worry. Worry is useless.
God is merciful and will hear your prayer."
— *Padre Pio*

"Grant me, O Lord my God, a mind to know you, a heart to seek you, wisdom to find you, conduct pleasing to you, faithful perseverance in waiting for you, and a hope of finally embracing you. Amen."
— *Thomas Aquinas*

"Love people who hate you. Pray for people who have wronged you. It won't just change their life…it'll change yours."
— *Mandy Hale*

"There comes a time in your life, when you walk away from all the drama and people who create it. You surround yourself with people who make you laugh. Forget the bad and focus on the good. Love the people who treat you right, pray for the ones who do not. Life is too short to be anything but happy. Falling down is a part of life, getting back up is living."
— *José N. Harris*

"Go where your best prayers take you."
— *Frederick Buechner*

"For the happy man prayer is only a jumble of words, until the day when sorrow comes to explain to him the sublime language by means of which he speaks to God."
— *Alexandre Dumas*

"We have to pray with our eyes on God, not on the difficulties."
— *Oswald Chambers*

To gently push aside and silence the many voices that question my goodness and to trust that I will hear the voice of blessing-- that demands real effort. "
— *Henri J.M. Nouwen*

"Lord, when I feel that what I'm doing is insignificant and unimportant, help me to remember that everything I do is significant and important in your eyes, because you love me and you put me here, and no one else can do what I am doing in exactly the way I do it."
— *Brennan Manning*

"He who kneels the most, stands the best."
— *D.L. Moody*

"No man is greater than his prayer life. The pastor who is not praying is playing; the people who are not praying are straying. We have many organizers, but few agonizers; many players and payers, few pray-ers; many singers, few clingers; lots of pastors, few wrestlers; many fears, few tears; much fashion, little passion; many interferers, few intercessors; many writers, but few fighters. Failing here, we fail everywhere."
— *Leonard Ravenhill*

"God will answer you prayers better than you think. Of course, one will not always get exactly what he has asked for....We all have sorrows and disappointments, but one must never forget that, if commended to God, they will issue in good.... His own solution is far better than any we could conceive."
— *Fanny J. Crosby*

"People who fit don't seek. The seekers are those who don't fit."
— *Shannon L. Alder*

"Today Lord I am going to do my best with Your help and for Your glory. I realize that there are many different people in the world with a variety of opinions and expectations. I will concentrate on being a God-pleaser and not a self-pleaser or man-pleaser. The rest I leave in Your hands lord. Grant me favor with You and with men and continue transforming me into the image of Your dear Son. Thank You Lord."
— *Joyce Meyer*

"I marveled at the beauty of all life and savored the power and possibilities of my imagination. In these rare moments, I prayed, I danced, and I analyzed. I saw that life was good and bad, beautiful and ugly. I understood that I had to dwell on the good and beautiful in order to keep my imagination, sensitivity, and gratitude intact. I knew it would not be easy to maintain this perspective. I knew I would often twist and turn, bend and crack a little, but I also knew that…I would never completely break."
— *Maria Nhambu*

"Your prayer for someone may or may not change them, but it always changes YOU."
— *Craig Groeschel*

"the real "work" of prayer is to become silent and listen to the voice that says good things about me.

"If my eyes have pain, I close them; If my body aches, I rest it; If my heart breaks, I mend it; If my soul is lost, I pray for it"
— *Jeremy Aldana*

"Perfect prayer does not consist in many words, silent remembering and pure intention raises the heart to that supreme Power."
— Amit Ray

"Pray for the dead and fight like hell for the living."
— *Mother Jones*

"…the three things I cannot change are the past, the truth, and you."
— *Anne Lamott*

"The easiest way to get touch with this universal power is through silent Prayer. Shut your eyes, shut your mouth, and open your heart. This is the golden rule of prayer. Prayer should be soundless words coming forth from the center of your heart filled with love."
— *Amit Ray*

"We never know how God will answer our prayers, but we can
expect that He will get us involved in His plan for the answer.
If we are true intercessors, we must be ready to take part in
God's work on behalf of the people for whom we pray."
— *Corrie ten Boom*

"Your desire is your prayer. Picture the fulfillment
of your desire now and feel its reality and
you will experience the joy of the answered."
— *Dr. Joseph Murphy*

"Prayer makes your heart bigger, until it is capable of
containing the gift of God himself. Prayer begets faith, faith
begets love, and love begets service on behalf of the poor."
— *Mother Teresa*

"Prayer is the soul's sincere desire. Your desire is
your prayer. It comes out of your deepest needs
and it reveals the things you want in life."
— *Joseph Murphy*

"Where did you get the idea you aren't allowed to petition
the universe with prayer? You are part of this universe, Liz.
You're a constituent--you have every entitlement to participate
in the actions of the universe, and to let your feelings be known.
So, put your opinion out there. Make your case. Believe
me--it will at least be taken into consideration."
— *Elizabeth Gilbert*

"I can do this… I can start over. I can save my own
life and I'm never going to be alone as long as
I have stars to wish on and people to still love."
— *Jennifer Elisabeth*

"Fear is the glue that keeps you stuck.
Faith is the solvent that sets you free."
— *Shannon L. Alder*

"For me, prayer is a surge of the heart; it is a simple
look turned toward heaven, it is a cry of recognition
and of love, embracing both trial and joy."
— *St. Therese of Lisieux*

"I found my God in music and the arts, with writers like
Hermann Hesse, and musicians like Muddy Waters, Howlin'
Wolf, and Little Walter. In some way, in some form, my God
was always there, but now I have learned to talk to him."
— *Eric Clapton*

"God, teach me to be patient, teach me to go slow,
Teach me how to wait on You when my way I do not know.

Teach me sweet forbearance when things do not go right
So I remain unruffled when others grow uptight.

Teach me how to quiet my racing, rising heart
So I might hear the answer You are trying to impart.

Teach me to let go, dear God, and pray undisturbed until
My heart is filled with inner peace and I learn to know your will."
— *Helen Steiner Rice*

"Prayer is beyond any question the highest activity
of the human soul. Man is at his greatest and highest
when upon his knees he comes face to face with God."
— *Martyn Lloyd-Jones*

"O heavenly Father,
protect and bless all things
that have breath: guard them
from all evil and let them sleep in peace."
— *Albert Schweitzer*

"Writing is prayer."
— *Franz Kafka*

"Lord, make me an instrument of your peace;
where there is hatred, let me sow love;
when there is injury, pardon;
where there is doubt, faith;
where there is despair, hope;
where there is darkness, light;
and where there is sadness, joy.
Grant that I may not so much seek
to be consoled as to console;
to be understood, as to understand,
to be loved as to love;
for it is in giving that we receive,
it is in pardoning that we are pardoned,
and it is in dying [to ourselves] that we are born to eternal life."
— *Francis Of Assisi*

"Let your life reflect the faith you have in God.
Fear nothing and pray about everything.
Be strong, trust God's word, and trust the process."
— *Germany Kent*

"When you touch the celestial in your heart, you will
realize that the beauty of your soul is so pure, so vast
and so devastating that you have no option but to merge
with it. You have no option but to feel the rhythm
of the universe in the rhythm of your heart."
— *Amit Ray*

"Pray, and let God worry."
— *Martin Luther*

"No one can believe how powerful prayer is and
what it can effect, except those who have learned it by
experience. Whenever I have prayed earnestly, I have
been heard and have obtained more than I prayed for.
God sometimes delays, but He always comes."
— *Martin Luther*

"What the Church needs to-day is not more machinery or better, not new organizations or more and novel methods, but men whom the Holy Ghost can use -- men of prayer, men mighty in prayer. The Holy Ghost does not flow through methods, but through men. He does not come on machinery, but on men. He does not anoint plans, but men -- men of prayer."
— *E.M. Bounds*

"Let this time in your life cut you open and drain all of the things that are holding you back. I'm going to help you forgive the things that you won't let yourself forget."
— *Jennifer Elisabeth*

"Prayer is not overcoming God's reluctance. It is laying hold of His willingness."
— *Martin Luther*

"Each time, before you intercede, be quiet first, and worship God in His glory. Think of what He can do, and how He delights to hear the prayers of His redeemed people. Think of your place and privilege in Christ, and expect great things!"
— *Andrew Murray*

"The Christian should work as if all depended upon him, and pray as if it all depended upon God."
— *Charles H. Spurgeon*

"Lord, make me a blessing to someone today."
— *Jan Karon*

"Prayer will make a man cease from sin, or sin will entice a man to cease from prayer."
— *John Bunyan*

"If you want to protect me, prayer is just as powerful a weapon as that gun you carry."
— *Karen Witemeyer*

"We tend to be preoccupied by our problems when we have a heightened sense of vulnerability and a diminished sense of power. Today, see each problem as an invitation to prayer."
— *John Ortberg*

"Pray to catch the bus, then run as fast as you can."
— *Julia Cameron*

"The only difference between a wish and a prayer is that you're at the mercy of the universe for the first, and you've got some help with the second."
— *Jodi Picoult*

"The best way to obtain truth and wisdom is not to ask from books, but to go to God in prayer, and obtain divine teaching."
— *Joseph Smith Jr.*

"When man is with God in awe and love, then he is praying."
— *Karl Rahner*

"Communicating with God is the most extraordinary experience imaginable, yet at the same time it's the most natural one of all, because God is present in us at all times. Omniscient, omnipotent, personal-and loving us without conditions. We are connected as One through our divine link with God."
— *Eben Alexander*

"I'll pray that you grow up a brave man in a brave country. I will pray you find a way to be useful.

I'll pray, and then I'll sleep."
— *Marilynne Robinson*

"When I pray for another person, I am praying for God to open my eyes so that I can see that person as God does, and then enter into the stream of love that God already directs toward that person."
— *Philip Yancey*

> "Groanings which cannot be uttered are often prayers which cannot be refused."
> — *C.H. Spurgeon*

"When we retire at night, we constructively review our day. Were we resentful, selfish, dishonest or afraid? Do we owe an apology? Have we kept something to ourselves which should be discussed with another person at once? Were we kind and loving toward all? What could we have done better? Were we thinking of ourselves most of the time? Or were we thinking of what we could do for others, of what we could pack into the stream of life? But we must be careful not to drift into worry, remorse or morbid reflection, for that would diminish our usefulness to others. After making our review we ask God's forgiveness and inquire what corrective measures should be taken.

On awakening let us think about the twenty-four hours ahead. We consider our plans for the day. Before we begin, we ask God to direct our thinking, especially asking that it be divorced from self-pity, dishonest or self-seeking motives. Under these conditions we can employ our mental faculties with assurance, for after all God gave us brains to use. Our thought-life will be placed on a much higher plane when our thinking is cleared of wrong motives.

In thinking about our day we may face indecision. We may not be able to determine which course to take. Here we ask God for inspiration, an intuitive thought or a decision. We relax and take it easy. We don't struggle. We are often surprised how the right answers come after we have tried this for a while.

What used to be the hunch or the occasional inspiration gradually becomes a working part of the mind. Being still inexperienced and having just made conscious contact with God, it is not probable that we are going to be inspired at all times. We might pay for this presumption in all sorts of absurd actions and ideas. Nevertheless, we find that our thinking will, as time passes, be more and more on the plane of inspiration. We come to rely upon it.

We usually conclude the period of meditation with a prayer that we be shown all through the day what our next step is to be, that we be given whatever we need to take care of such problems. We ask especially for freedom from self-will, and are careful to make no request for ourselves only. We may ask for ourselves, however, if others will be helped. We are careful never to pray for our own selfish ends. Many of us have wasted a lot of time doing that and it doesn't work. You can easily see why."
— *Bill Wilson*

~ God be in my head and in my understanding.
God be in my eyes and in my looking.
God be in my mouth and in my speaking.
God be in my tongue and in my tasting.
God be in my lips and in my greeting.
~ God be in my nose and in my smelling/inhaling.
God be in my ears and in my hearing.
God be in my neck and in my humbling.
God be in my shoulders and in my bearing.
God be in my back and in my standing.
~ God be in my arms and in my reaching/receiving.
God be in my hands and in my working.
God be in my legs and in my walking.
God be in my feet and in my grounding.
God be in my knees and in my relating
~ God be in my gut and in my feeling.
God be in my bowels and in my forgiving.
God be in my loins and in my swiving.
God be in my lungs and in my breathing.
God be in my heart and in my loving.
~ God be in my skin and in my touching.
God be in my flesh and in my paining/pining.
God be in my blood and in my living.
God be in my bones and in my dying.
God be at my end and at my reviving."
— *Caroline Myss*

"God help us to live slowly:
To move simply:
To look softly:
To allow emptiness:
To let the heart create for us.
Amen."
— *Michael Leunig*

"Lord, teach me to be generous;
Teach me to serve you as you deserve;
To give and not to count the cost;
To fight and not to heed the wounds;
To toil, and not to seek for rest;
To labor, and not to ask for reward -
except to know that I am doing your will."
— *St. Ignatius of Loyola*

"Lord, to the degree I don't want to do this, bless me."
— *Luci Swindoll*

"Work as if everything depended upon work and
pray as if everything depended upon prayer."
— *William Booth*

"When I cannot read, when I cannot think,
when I cannot even pray, I can trust."
— *Hudson Taylor*

"Anyone who is having troubles should pray. Anyone who is happy should sing praises. Anyone who is sick should call the church's elders. They should pray for and pour oil on the person in the name of the Lord. And the prayer that is said with faith will make the sick person well; the Lord will heal that person. And if the person has sinned, the sins will be forgiven. Confess your sins to each other and pray for each other so God can heal you. When a believing person prays, great things happen."
— *James 5:13-16 (King James Version)*

"Imagine that Jesus is calling you today. He extends
a second invitation to accept His Father's love. And
maybe you answer, "Oh, I know that. It's old hat.""

And God answers, 'No, that's what you don't know. You don't
know how much I love you. The moment you think you
understand is the moment you do not understand. I am God,
not man. You tell others about Me - your words are glib. My
words are written in the blood of My only Son. The next time
you preach about My love with such obnoxious familiarity,
I may come and blow your whole prayer meeting apart.

Did you know that every time you tell
Me you love Me, I say thank you?"
— *Brennan Manning*

"A prayer couched in the words of the soul,
is far more powerful than any ritual."
— *Paulo Coelho*

"I have always been a firm believer in God and the power of
prayer, though to be honest, my faith has made for alist of
questions I definitely want answered after I'm gone."
— *Nicholas Sparks*

"The goal of prayer is to live all of my life and speak all
of my words in the joyful awareness of the presence of God.
Prayer becomes real when we grasp the reality and goodness
of God's constant presence with 'the real me.' Jesus lived
his everyday life in conscious awareness of his Father."
— *John Ortberg*

"Not being changed by prayer is sort of life standing
in the middle of a spring rain without getting wet.
It's hard to stand in the center of God's acceptance
and love without getting it all over you."
— *Steve Brown*

"We can be tired, weary and emotionally distraught,
but after spending time alone with God, we find that
He injects into our bodies energy, power and strength."
— *Charles Stanley*

"It is of great importance, when we begin to practice prayer,
not to let ourselves be frightened by our own thoughts."
— *Santa Teresa de Jesús*

"Sometimes the best answers to prayer
are the ones God doesn't answer."
— *Robin Jones Gunn*

"No one particular religion has been able to secure the exclusive
rights for the power of prayer. No matter who you are,
we all have the ability to take advantage of this amazing and
wonderful power. Once you realize this, you will then
be filled with the desire to help others realize this as well.
More and more people are resonating with this understanding,
and this could result in a more wonderful future for mankind."
— *Masaru Emoto*

"Writing, music, sculpting, painting, and prayer! These are the
three things that are most closely related! Writers, musicians,
sculptors, painters, and the faithful are the ones who make things
out of nothing. Everybody else, they make things out of something,
they have materials! But a written work can be done with nothing,
it can begin in the soul! A musical piece begins with a harmony in
the soul, a sculpture begins with a formless, useless piece of rock
chiseled and formed and molded into the thing that was first
conceived in the sculptor's heart! A painting can be carried inside
the mind for a lifetime, before ever being put onto paper or
canvass! And a prayer! A prayer is a thought, a remembrance, a
whisper, a communion, that is from the soul going to what cannot
be seen, yet it can move mountains! And so I believe that these
five things are interrelated, these five kinds of people are kin."
— *C. JoyBell C.*

"To be a Christian without prayer is no more
possible than to be alive without breathing."
— *Martin Luther King Jr*

"Prayer will never do our work for us; what it will do
is to strengthen us for work which must be done."
— *William Barclay*

"Praying and sinning will never live together in the same heart.
Prayer will consume sin, or sin will choke prayer."
— *J.C. Ryle*

"The heart overflows with gladness, and leaps and dances for the joy
it has found in God. In this experience the Holy Spirit is active, and
has taught us in the flash of a moment the deep secret of joy. You will
have as much joy and laughter in life as you have faith in God."
— *Martin Luther*

"Prayer is like water - something you can't imagine
has the strength or power to do any good, and yet
give it time and it can change the lay of the land."
— *Jodi Picoult*

"If I ask God to punish my enemy with vengeful prayers,
then He is fair to allow the enemy to do the same for me."
— *Toba Beta*

"Prayer can solve more problems, alleviate more suffering, prevent
more transgression, and bring about greater peace and contentment
in the human soul than can be obtained in any other way."
— *Thomas S. Monson*

"The most important thing we can pray about for others is that they
will know God better and that He will help them understand His will,
grow in spiritual wisdom, and live lives that honor Him. We can pray
that they will become more like Him and bear the fruit of His Spirit."
— *Stormie Omartian*

"Pray the largest prayers. You cannot think a prayer so large that God, in answering it, will not wish you had made it larger. Pray not for crutches but for wings."
— *Phillips Brooks*

"We do not want to be beginners [at prayer], but let us be convinced of the fact that we will never be anything but beginners, all our life!"
— *Thomas Merton*

"The 3 most powerful resources you have available to you : love, prayer and forgiveness."
— *H. Jackson Brown, Jr.*

"You are angry at the God you were taught to believe in as a child. The God who is supposed to watch over you and protect you, who answers your prayers and forgives your sins. This God is just a story. Religions try to capture God, but God is beyond religion. The true God lies beyond our comprehension. We can't understand His will; He can't be explained in a book. He didn't abandon us and He will not save us. He has nothing to do with our being here. God does not change. He simply is. I don't pray to God for forgiveness or favors, I only pray to be closer to Him, and when I pray, I fill my heart with love. When I pray this way, I know that God is love. When I feel that love, I remember that we don't need angels or a heaven, because we are a part of God already."
— *Nando Parrado*

"Prayer is the most powerful resource we have in this life; yet, many only turn to it as a last resort. When unbelievers pray for repentance of sin and ask for God's forgiveness, prayer is the spiritual dynamite that obliterates the darkness and despair of a sin-soaked soul."
— *Franklin Graham*

"A man may study because his brain is hungry for knowledge, even Bible knowledge. But he prays because his soul is hungry for God."
— *Leonard Ravenhill*

"Dear God

Please take away my pain and despair of yesterday and any unpleasant memories and replace them with Your glorious promise of new hope. Show me a fresh HS-inspired way of relating to negative things that have happened. I ask You for the mind of Christ so I can discern Your voice from the voice of my past. I pray that former rejection and deep hurts will not color what I see and hear now.

Help me to see all the choices I have ahead of me that can alter the direction of my life. I ask You to empower me to let go of the painful events and heartaches that would keep me bound. Thank You for Your forgiveness that You have offered to me at such a great price. Pour it into my heart so I can relinquish bitterness hurts and disappointments that have no place in my life. Please set me free to forgive those who have sinned against me and caused me pain and also myself. Open my heart to receive Your complete forgiveness and amazing grace. You have promised to bind up my wounds [Psa 147:3] and restore my soul [Psa 23:3].

Help me to relinquish my past surrender to You my present and move to the future You have prepared for me. I ask You to come into my heart and make me who You would have me to be so that I might do Your will here on earth. I thank You Lord for all that's happened in my past and for all I have become through those experiences. I pray You will begin to gloriously renew my present."
— *Sue Augustine*

"Love is the only prayer I know."
— *Marion Zimmer Bradley*

"Why we pray matters as much as what we pray."
— *Marsha DuCille*

"The great thing in prayer is to feel that we are putting our supplications into the bosom of omnipotent love."
— *Andrew Murray*

"The primary purpose of prayer is not to make requests. The primary purpose is to praise, to sing, to chant. Because the essence of prayer is a song, and man cannot live without a song.

Prayer may not save us. But prayer may make us worthy of being saved."
— *Abraham Joshua Heschel*

"God takes everyone he loves through a desert. It is his cure for our wandering hearts, restlessly searching for a new Eden...

The best gift of the desert is God's presence... The protective love of the Shepherd gives me courage to face the interior journey."
— *Paul E. Miller*

"Spirituality without a prayer life is no spirituality at all, and it will not last beyond the first defeats. Prayer is an opening of the self so that the Word of God can break in and make us new. Prayer unmasks. Prayer converts. Prayer impels. Prayer sustains us on the way. Pray for the grace it will take to continue what you would like to quit."
— *Joan Chittister*

"Learn to pray. Pray often. Pray in your mind, in your heart. Pray on your knees. Prayer is your personal key to heaven. The lock is on your side of the veil. And I have learned to conclude all my prayers with 'Thy will be done' (Matthew 6:10; see also Luke 11:2; 3 Nephi 13:10)."
— *Boyd K. Packer*

"Don't pray when it rains if you don't pray when the sun shines."
— *Satchel Paige*

"[Prayer] is the link between God's inexhaustible resources and people's needs...God is the source of power, but we are the instrument He uses to link the two together."
— *Charles Stanley*

"Sometimes when we say "God is silent," what's really going on is that he hasn't told the story the way we wanted it told. He will be silent when we want him to fill in the blanks of the story we are creating. But with his own stories, the ones we live in, he is seldom silent."
— *Paul E. Miller*

"One must pray first, but afterwards one must help oneself. God does not care for cowards."
— *Ouida*

"One who prays ceaselessly is one who combines prayer with work and work with prayer."
— *Origen*

"Don't forget to pray today because God did not forget to wake you up this morning."
— *Oswald Chambers*

"If you don't pray often, you won't gain a love for praying. Prayer is work, and therefore it is not very appealing to our natural sensibilities. But the simple rule for prayer is this: Begin praying and your taste for prayer will increase. The more you pray, the more you will acquire the desire for prayer, the energy for prayer, and the sense of purpose in prayer."
— *Leslie Ludy*

"Something, somewhere, knows what's best for me and promises to keep sending me people and experiences to light my way as long as I live in gratitude and keep paying attention to the signs."
— *Jennifer Elisabeth*

"You asked the Holy Spirit for a miracle, and now that you've got one you're trying to argue it away. People who don't believe in miracles shouldn't pray for them."
— *David Wilkerson*

"Really, there was only one sensible thing to do. Stay the course. Pray it through, day by day, minute by minute. The Lord had an answer and it would surely come."
— *Janice Hanna*

"They who reach down into the depths of life where, in the stillness, the voice of God is heard, have the stabilizing power which carries them poised and serene through the hurricane of difficulties."
— *Spencer W. Kimball*

"I guarantee you that after you die you will not say 'I spent too much time praying; I wish I had watched more TV instead."
— *Peter Kreeft*

"The value of consistent prayer is not that [God] will hear us, but that we will hear Him."
— *William McGill*

"After much prayer, careful study and reliance on the Holy Spirit, I have concluded this about Christ's intercession for us. Jesus died on the cross to purchase peace with God for me – and He is in heaven now to maintain that peace, for me and in me."
— *David Wilkerson*

"The single most important piece of advice about prayer is one word: Begin!"
— *Peter Kreeft*

"I am thankful that there are those among us who have sacrificed dearly on behalf of us. And I ardently pray to God that I might be less like myself and more like them."
— *Craig D. Lounsbrough*

"The woman who makes a sweet, beautiful home, filling it with love and prayer and purity, is doing something better than anything else her hands could find to do beneath the skies."
— *J.R. Miller*

"Why do you pray?" he asked me, after a moment.

Why did I pray? A strange question.
Why did I live? Why did I breathe?

"I don't know why," I said, even more
disturbed and ill at ease. "I don't know why."

After that day I saw him often. He explained to me with great insistence that every question possessed a power that did not lie in the answer. "Man raises himself toward God by the questions he asks Him," he was fond of repeating. "That is the true dialogue. Man questions God and God answers. But we don't understand His answers. We can't understand them. Because they come from the depths of the soul, and they stay there until death. You will find the true answers, Eliezer, only within yourself!"

"And why do you pray, Moshe?" I asked him.
"I pray to the God within me that He will give
me the strength to ask Him the right questions."
— *Elie Wiesel*

"Perhaps all the good that ever has come here has come because
people prayed it into the world."
— *Wendell Berry*

"Temptation is stronger in the minds of people who are in doubt.
Prayer makes it weaker."
— *Toba Beta*

"The world is my church. My actions are my prayer. My
behavior is my creed."
— *Steve Maraboli*

"I don't pray because it makes sense to pray. I pray
because my life doesn't make sense without prayer."
— *Noah Benshea*

"I came to set fire to the earth. And I am watchful that the fire grow.
May the fire of love grow in our hearts.
May the fire of transformation glow in our movements.
May the fire of purification burn away our sins.
May the fire of justice guide our steps.
May the fire of wisdom illuminate our paths.
May the fire that spreads over the Earth never be extinguished."
— *Paulo Coelho*

"Self-will and prayer are both ways of getting things done. At the center of self-will is me, carving a world in my image, but at the center of prayer is God, carving me in his Son's image."
— *Paul E. Miller*

"Keep me safe, keep me from harm, keep me in your loving arms."
— *Mindy Starns Clark*

"Nothing but prayer can make saints because nothing but God can make saints, and we meet God in prayer. Prayer is the hospital for souls where we meet Doctor God."
— *Peter Kreeft*

"Prayer not only teaches and strengthens one for work, work teaches and strengthens one for prayer."
— *Andrew Murray*

"Prayer does change things, all kinds of things. But the most important thing it changes is us. As we engage in this communion with God more deeply and come to know the One with whom we are speaking more intimately, that growing knowledge of God reveals to us all the more brilliantly who we are and our need to change in conformity to Him. Prayer changes us profoundly."
— *R.C. Sproul*

"Even the smallest shift in perspective can bring about the greatest healing."
— *Joshua Kai*

"It is of great significance if there is a person who truly prays in a family. Prayer attracts God's Grace and all the members of the family feel it, even those whose hearts have grown cold. Pray always."
— *Elder Thaddeus of Vitovnica*

"Our forgiving love toward men is the evidence of God's forgiving love in us. It is a necessary condition of the prayer of faith."
— *Andrew Murray*

"She knew that oftentimes hurtful people were hurting people, so she determined to pray for them all the more."
— *J.E.B. Spredemann*

"It has been said by many great Christians that prayer is our secret weapon. If we desire to be free from every enemy stronghold over our lives and fully fortified to live the superhuman existences God intended us to live, then we must learn how to pray."
— *Leslie Ludy*

"Forgiveness is how we free ourselves from the emotional weight that has us bound."
— *Marsha DuCille*

"The greatest thing anyone can do for God and man is pray. It is not the only thing; but it is the chief thing. The great people of the earth today are the people who pray. I do not mean those who talk about prayer; not those who can explain about prayer; but I mean those people who take time and pray"
— *S.D. Gordon*

"The most powerful thought is a prayerful thought. When I'm praying for you, I am praying for my own peace of mind. I can only have for myself what I am willing to wish for you."
— *Marianne Williamson*

"Where there is prayer, the fallen spirits have no power."
— Elder Thaddeus of Vitovnica, Our Thoughts Determine Our Lives: The Life and Teachings of Elder Thaddeus of Vitovnica

"Only when we can accept God as he is can we give up the desire for spiritual experiences that we can feel."
— *Thomas Keating*

"As long as we have unsolved problems, unfulfilled desires, and a mustard seed of faith, we have all we need for a vibrant prayer life."
— *John Ortberg*

"Prayer is not a means of removing the unknown and predictable elements in life, but rather a way of including the unknown and unpredictable in the outworking of the grace of God in our lives."
— *Phillip Yancey*

"To my surprise, I had not just doodled, I had prayed (I drew new shapes and names of each friend and focused on the person whose name stared at me from the paper). I had though OF each person as I drew but not ABOUT each person. I could just sit with them in a variation on stillness. I could hold them in prayer."
— *Sybil MacBeth*

"Loving someone is waking up a little bit earlier than they do so you can pray for their day."
— *Melissa Z*

"What have you gained since you haven't prayed? What will you lose if you pray?"
— *Agu, Jaachynma N.E.*

"I really believe that there is an invisible red thread tied between him and me, and that it has stretched an tangled for years — across oceans and lifetimes. I know that it won't break because our souls are tied."
— *Jennifer Elisabeth*

"If we allow our "high creativity" to remain alive, we will never be bored. We can pray, standing in line at the super market. Or we can be lost in awe at all the people around us, their lives full of glory and tragedy, and suddenly we will have the beginnings of a painting, a story, a song."
— *Madeleine L'Engle*

"Prayer is a protective shield."
— *Lailah Gifty Akita*

"Trying to describe what I do in prayer would be like telling the world how I make love to my wife. "
— *J.I. Packer*

"The wish to pray is a prayer in itself."
— *George Bernanos*

"Everything you do is connected to who you are as a person and, in turn, creates the person you are becoming. Everything you do affects those you love. All of life is covenant.

Imbedded in the idea of prayer is a richly textured view of the world where all of life is organized around invisible bonds or covenants that knit us together. Instead of a fixed world, we live in our Father's world, a world built for divine relationships between people where, because of the Good News, tragedies become comedies and hope is born."
— *Paul E. Miller*

"Prayer is helpful. It will help you feel peaceful."
— *Gift Gugu Mona*

"As a prayer popper, I stay in touch with God. I send lots of spiritual postcards. Little bits and bytes of adoration, supplication, and information attached prayer darts speed in God's direction all day long."
— *Sybil MacBeth*

"One, just one, but definitely one of the great benefits of private prayer is that you can't hide from your motives. In corporate prayer, we can sound like "all that". We can blow Jesus smoke like nobody's bizness in a crowd but, get alone with Him, and He won't let you get away with the fake stuff. Try blowing Jesus smoke in your prayer closet and you'll cough on it every time. Truth? That penetrating gaze of His hurts, but afterwards, it never fails to heal."
— *Shellie Rushing Tomlinson*

"…be awake to the Life
that is loving you and
sing your prayer, laugh your prayer,
dance your prayer, run
and weep and sweat your prayer,
sleep your prayer, eat your prayer,
paint, sculpt, hammer, and read your prayer,
sweep, dig, rake, drive and hoe your prayer,
garden and farm and build and clean your prayer,
wash, iron, vacuum, sew, embroider and pickle your prayer,
compute, touch, bend and fold but never delete
or mutilate your prayer.

Learn and play your prayer,
work and rest your prayer,
fast and feast your prayer,
argue, talk, whisper, listen and shout your prayer,
groan and moan and spit and sneeze your prayer,
swim and hunt and cook your prayer,
digest and become your prayer,
release and recover your prayer,
breathe your prayer,
be your prayer"
— *Alla Renee Bozarth*

"A concentrated mind and a sitting body make for bette prayer than a kneeling body and a mind half asleep."
— *C.S. Lewis*

"Prayer is thinking deeply about something in the presence of God."
— *Wayne Cordeiro*

"My prayer for you today is that you experience the Love that God has for you in such a profound, childlike way that your perspective is completely transformed. As you encounter circumstances in your life, from the trivial to the catastrophic, may you be more acutely aware of the magnitude of His love for you than the magnitude of the troubles you face."
— *Riisa Renee*

"There is no possibility like prayer."
— *Lailah Gifty Akita*

"We must never forget to pray, and to ask God to remember us when He is arranging things, so that we too may feel safe and have no anxiety about what is going to happen."
— *Johanna Spyri*

"Men may spurn our appeals, reject our message, oppose our arguments, despise our persons, but they are helpless against our prayers."
— *J. Sidlow Baxter*

"I believe God has heard my prayers. He will make it manifest in His own good time that He has heard me. I have recorded my petitions that when God has answered them, His name will be glorified."
— *George Muller*

"Keep your prayer simple. Whatever confuses or complicates prayer is probably best forgotten."
— *Mark Link*

"Prayer is not itself powerful; it is not magic. But its power is unlimited in that the child of God calls on a Father of unlimited goodness and ability."
— *Peter H. Davids*

"Prayer is the force as real as terrestrial gravity. As a physician, I have seen men, after all other therapy had failed, lifted out of disease and melancholy by the serene effort of prayer. Only in prayer do we achieve that complete and harmonious assembly of body, mind and spirit which gives the frail human reed its unshakable strength."
— *Alexis Carrel*

"Prayer [is] the quiet, persistent living of our life of desire and faith in the presence of our God."
— *Andrew Murray*

"Prayer is a private communion with God."
— *Lailah Gifty Akita*

"Prayer is asking God to incarnate, to get dirty in your life. Yes, the eternal God scrubs floors. For sure we know he washes feet. So take Jesus at his word. Ask him. Tell him what you want. Get dirty. Write out your prayer requests; don't mindlessly drift through life on the American narcotic of busyness. If you try to seize the day, the day will eventually break you. Seize the corner of his garment and don't let go until he blesses you. He will reshape the day."
— *Paul E. Miller*

"When confronted with suffering that won't go away or with even a minor problem, we instinctively focus on what is missing,...not on the Master's hand. Often when you think everything has gone wrong, it's just that you're in the middle of a story. If you watch the stories God is weaving in your life, you... will begin to see the patterns. You'll become a poet, sensitive to your Father's voice."
— *Paul E. Miller*

"Jesus kept it simple. The lesson wasn't complicated. 'I speak; you believe My word; your son will be fine.' We complicate what God has made simple by seeing the world through human eyes. We want to see in order to believe and presume that our limitations are His."
— *Charles R. Swindoll*

"HARRINGTON: And God hears your prayer,
doesn't he? We hear Joy's getting better.

LEWIS: That's not why I pray, Harry. I pray because I can't help myself. I pray because I'm helpless. I pray because the need flows out of me, waking and sleeping. It doesn't change God, it changes me."
— *William Nicholson*

"I recall hearing one of my professors in seminary
say that one of the best tests of a person's
theology was the effect it has on one's prayers."
— *John Piper*

"To be in the presence of God, prayer is necessary."
— *Lailah Gifty Akita*

"Prayer without study would be empty.
Study without prayer would be blind."
— *Karl Barth*

"It is good for us to have trials and troubles at times, for they often remind us that we are on probation and ought not to hope in any worldly thing. It is good for us sometimes to suffer contradiction, to be misjudged by men even though we do well and mean well. These things help us to be humble and shield us from vainglory. When to all outward appearances men give us no credit, when they do not think well of us, then we are more inclined to seek God Who sees our hearts. Therefore, a man ought to root himself so firmly in God that he will not need the consolations of men."
— *Thomas à Kempis*

"My prayer is an attitude of pure gratitude for having the opportunity to experience life on this earth with all its pain, heartache, worry, and turmoil; coupled with this gratitude is the thankfulness for just having the opportunity to have lived. That is fairly easy on good days but difficult when life puts rocks and boulders in the road."
— *David W Earle*

"Choose to view life through God's eyes. This will not be easy because it doesn't come naturally to us. We cannot do this on our own. We have to allow God to elevate our vantage point. Start by reading His Word, the Bible...Pray and ask God to transform your thinking. Let Him do what you cannot. Ask Him to give you an eternal, divine perspective."
— *Charles R. Swindoll*

"Pray each morning and each night.
Talk to God and be polite.
Tell Him what you're grateful for.
Leave your troubles at His door.

Share your wishes, needs, and hopes.
Ask God how to bravely cope.
Tell Him all you learned today.
Say the things you need to say.

Beg forgiveness for your sins.
Pray to live with Him again.
Speak with earnest heart and soul.
He will listen. This I know.

For prayer is hope put to the test.
And hope is faith in what is best.
Faith is power to do great things.
Thus, prayer is faith's enabling wings."
— *Richelle E. Goodrich*

"Prayer is an insurance policy that you can never lapse on."
— *The Prolific Penman*

"In order to resist fear and discouragement, it is necessary that through prayer - through a personal experience of God re-encountered, recognized and loved in prayer - we taste and see how good the Lord is (Psalm 34)."
— *Jacques Philippe*

"Hope and prayer are the fuel of all human souls, go for it and God will do a trick to shine in any situation."
— *Santosh Kumar (San)*

"There is no peace without prayer."
— *Lailah Gifty Akita*

"Ask. Trust. Give thanks. Simple right?"
— *Dawn Gluskin*

"Victories are won while on your knees! Keep praying for those who rise up against you. Fear not. The Lord has rectified the problem. Prayer is POWERFUL!!"
— *Anita R. Sneed-Carter*

"I wanted my sons to know that, whatever kinds of prayers we utter, not matter how wretched, God hears them, even when we pray badly."
— *Wendy Murray*

"Prayer is my chief work; by it I carry on all else. Prayer is the nearest approach to God and the highest enjoyment of him that we are capable of in this life. It is the noblest exercise of the soul. It is the most exalted use of our best faculties. It is the highest imitation of the blessed beings of heaven."
— *William Laws*

"A passionate prayer with a burning desire, pushed from within, any kind of prayer, that you are lost in the moment of praying is the prayer that opens heavens."
— *Anikor Daniel*

Praying into a bank of fog requires alot of effort. I wanted an image to focus on when I prayed. I wanted something to pray *to*. but I couldn't go back to that old man. He was too closely associated with all I'd left behind."
— *Margaret McGee*

"The biggest lie we fall for is that it doesn't matter. Your opinion doesn't matter. Your choices don't matter. Your influence doesn't matter. Your existence doesn't matter. You don't matter. It is the worst, most destructive lie we ever believe, and in consequence it wreaks extensive damage to more lives than your own. Don't fall for that evil lie. Don't forget that everything about you absolutely does matter."
— *Richelle E. Goodrich*

"Our attitudes are like uniform,
they disclose who we are."
— *Marsha DuCille*

"Prayer is a pillar that helps you to stand in times of storm."
— *Gift Gugu Mona*

"All stories are, in some form, prayers."
— *Brian Doyle*

I am continuing to believe BIG
and to pray BIG and work BIG!
— *T.J. Rohleder*

"My life is a prayer."
— *Joe Baker*

"Positivity = Teflon:

The more you pray to God –
turn things over to him and his power –
focus on the positive aspects of life –
and the positive messages of spirituality,
the more positive you will be and
the more power you will have to
not let the negativity stick to you.

The more you focus on the negative
and don't turn things over to God,
the more resentful and bitter and cynical
you will be, and the more negative situations
you will bring down on yourself. You will
actually attract even more of these things.

What you focus on expands, so
focus on positive prayer!"
— *Terence Storm*

"The whole function of the life of prayer is, then, to enlighten
and strengthen our conscience so that it not only knows
and perceives the outward, written precepts of the moral
and divine laws, but above all lives God's law in concrete
reality by perfect and continual union with His will."
— *Thomas Merton*

"Without prayer, there is no power to prevail."
— *Lailah Gifty Akita*

"All during that prison time I really lived
by prayer. Be in prayer always,
we're told, and back then I was."
— *Diet Eman*

"I pray to the birds because they remind me of
what I love rather than what I fear. And at the
end of my prayers, they teach me how to listen."
— *Terry Tempest Williams*

"Prayer is not mere wishing. It is asking –
with a will. ... It is energy. We turn to an
active Giver; therefore we go into action."
— *P.T. Forsyth*

"If it's worth doing, it's worth doing poorly.
(friend who is a priest said regarding prayer)"
— *Sybil MacBeth*

"Prayer leads to purity."
— *Lailah Gifty Akita*

"The best loved prayer is to love."
— *Gregory Wassil*

"Prayer is a communication tool that strengthens your relationship with God."
— *Gift Gugu Mona*

"We don't have a blessing shortage, we have a capacity crisis."
— *Andrena Sawyer*

"Thank God for the precious gift of prayer."
— *Lailah Gifty Akita*

"A spiritual life without prayer is like the gospel without Christ."
— *Henri J.M. Nouwen*

"The prayer of a pure heart never goes in vain!"
— *Dada J. P. Vaswani*

"For a prayer to be answered, a blessing or miracle to take place.

5 things need to change.
A change of heart
A change of mind
A change of faith
A change of attitude and
A change of behavior.

Proverbs 4:23 | Ephesians 4:23 | Hebrews 11:6"
— *DJ Kyos*

"Prayer is our yearning for God, the cry of our poverty and misery, stretching out toward the throne of His divine mercy."
— *Emmanuel D'Alzon*

"The value of consistent prayer is not that He will hear us, but that we will hear Him."
— *William McGill*

"Prayer is helplessness plus faith."
— *Bill Thrasher*

"Prayer is reaching out to God's hand so that you can understand His heart and plans for your life."
— *Gift Gugu Mona*

"Your personal truth is your gift to the world."
— *Jennifer Elisabeth*

"Prayer is the center of the Christian life. It is the only necessary thing. It is living with God in the here and now."
— *Henri J.M. Nouwen*

"Without pain, no prayer is said."
— *Lailah Gifty Akita*

"Lord Jesus, as it would please you bring me someone today whom I can serve."
— *Richard J. Foster*

"Prayer is the first defensive and best offense."
— *Craig D. Lounsbrough*

"Prayer is a path where there is none."
— *Noah Benshea*

"Prayer to God helps us to fight every difficulty."
— *Santosh Kumar*

"I think of prayers like tech support. Unless I get a person live on the phone, I'm not sure it's getting to anybody."
— *Mike Birbiglia*

"God always listens to my prayers,
I am able to see a clear picture now."
— *Santosh Kumar*

"As prayer warriors, we're not passive bystanders who let in whatever comes our way. Instead, we're spiritual gatekeepers who are commissioned to keep watch over what we think."
— *Marsha DuCille*

"Every word you speak is a prayer, or meditation of reinforcement which creates permanence."
— *Bryant McGill*

"We must never forget that everything that we do pens yet another line on the pages of the lives who are watching us. And once those lines are penned, there's no eraser with which to remove that which we wrote. Therefore, take time to pray before you pick up the pen."
— *Craig D. Lounsbrough*

"Amen' is like the Send button on an email."
— *Steve Toltz*

"Sweet Jesus
Let us live
In love together
As love forever"
— *A.D. Aliwat*

"When you're doing your best, at deeper level you will have total acceptance about the present situation and the outcome of your efforts. Prayer and divine intervention happens at that level."
— *Shunya*

"Faith and prayer are the vitamins of the soul; man
cannot live in health without them. ..."
— *William McGill*

"Never forget the three powerful resources you always
have available to you: love, prayer, and forgiveness."
— *H. Jackson Brown, Jr.*

"Sometimes you pray, and sometimes
you are the answered prayer."
— *Hannah Brencher*

"You might not be able to change your situation but prayer can."
— *Jerry Kinard*

"Love is the story and the prayer that matters the most."
— *Brian Doyle*

"My prayer is perpetual praise."
— *Lailah Gifty Akita*

"If a plane is too heavy, it can't fly safely. And if our spirits
are too loaded down, our lives are unable to soar."
— *Marsha DuCille*

"God, I give You my struggle with the future. With the present.
And the emptiness I feel when I think about what's to come.
Help me to rely on You every second of every day
and to know that You are always here with me."
— *Sunshine Rodgers*

"Let us pray to Allah to unite us for human mercy, instead of
dividing us all on what we believe. Ramadan Mubarak!"
— *Santosh Kumar*

"Perhaps thought really is prayer."
— *Ellis Peters*

"God always walks before you (to make a way);
walks beside you (to keep you strong); and
walks behind you (to catch you if you fall)."
— *Marsha DuCille*

"Pray like it all depends on God, but work like it all depends on you."
— *Dave Ramsey*

"You can do more than pray after you have prayed but
you cannot do more than pray until you have prayed."
— *S.D. Gordon*

"The act of prayer leads to the habit of prayer."
— *Lailah Gifty Akita*

"Don't expect a smile
if you're not smiling.
Don't expect a hug
if you fold your arms
across your chest.
Don't expect a laugh
if you're not laughing.
Don't expect success
if you fail to do
your very best.

Don't expect to hear
if you're not listening.
Don't expect to learn
if books pile up and
you never read.
Don't expect a friend
if you're not friendly.
Don't expect relief
if you turn your back
on those in need."
— *Richelle E. Goodrich*

"I pray to the birds because they remind me of what I love rather than what I fear. And at the end of my prayers, they teach me how to listen."
— *Terry Tempest Williams*

"Prayer is the ability to maintain a good connection between you and God."
— *Gift Gugu Mona*

"Everyone needs a support system, be it family, friends, coworkers, therapists, or religious leaders. We cannot do life alone and expect to keep mentally, emotionally, and spiritually healthy. Everyone needs some sort of support system on which to rely."
— *Richelle E. Goodrich*

"The correct prayer is therefore never a prayer of supplication (which means to request something), but a prayer of gratitude. When you thank God in advance for that which you choose to experience in your reality, you, in effect, acknowledge that it is there … in effect. Thankfulness is thus the most powerful statement to God; an affirmation that even before you ask, I have answered. Therefore never supplicate. Appreciate."
— *Neale Donald Walsch*

"Trying to pray is praying."
— *T.J. Rohleder*

# **CONCLUSION**

Our mission is to publish small books that deliver big value. I hope you've enjoyed this book. Small books offer something that big books can't. They're easy to read. They're ultra-portable. You can quickly glance at them and focus on the key ideas that are most important to you. It's hard to do that with a big book. Plus, digital books are easy to ignore. You can have 100s of them on your device and forget they're even there. With our small books, you can easily carry them with you and have them at your fingertips whenever you'd like. These small books can become a part of your life in ways that big books can't.

Our goal for each title is to deliver big value in ways that are important to you. We hope you get just one or two big ideas from this book that can change your life.

If you're happy with your purchase, please write a review on Amazon. Because many people only buy a book after reading some reviews, this helps other people make the decision to purchase this title. Who knows... Your review could play a small role in helping change someone else's life.

And let me leave you with this thought. One of my favorite restaurants has this saying hanging on their wall by the cash register: "If you're happy with your meal, please tell all your friends and family. If you're not happy, please tell us." If you love what you just read, share this book with everyone. And if there's something we could do to make it better, please reach out and let us know.

Sincerely,
***T.J. Rohleder***

P.S. If you enjoyed this small book and would like to purchase a few copies to share with other people, please reach out to us via our website (on back cover).

www.ingramcontent.com/pod-product-compliance
Lightning Source LLC
Chambersburg PA
CBHW020525030426
42337CB00011B/551